Resources for group time

Support for struggling readers

'Jasper's Beanstalk'

& other texts

Level 1/2 activities for 7–9 year olds

Kate Grant

Resources for group time

Contents

Author Kate Grant
Editor Clare Gallaher
Assistant editor Roanne Davis
Series designers Paul Cheshire and Joy Monkhouse
Illustrations Shirley Walker

Designed using Adobe Pagemaker

Published by Scholastic Ltd, Villiers House, Clarendon Avenue, Leamington Spa, Warwickshire CV32 5PR

Printed by Alden Group Ltd, Oxford

1 2 3 4 5 6 7 8 9 0   1 2 3 4 5 6 7 8 9 0

British Library Cataloguing-in-Publication Data
A catalogue record for this book is available from the British Library.

ISBN 0-439-01948-6

Acknowledgements

The publishers gratefully acknowledge permission to reproduce the following copyright material:

- **Andersen Press** for the use of a scanned front cover and permission to base activities on the book *Not Now, Bernard* by David McKee © 1980, David McKee (1980, Andersen Press). Black and white line illustrations first appeared in *Read & Respond: Not Now, Bernard* by Hilary Braund and Deborah Campbell, illustrations © 1999, David McKee (1999, Scholastic Ltd).
- **John Foster** for the use of 'Sand' from *Four O'Clock Friday* by John Foster © 1991, John Foster (1991, OUP).
- **Hodder and Stoughton Ltd** for the use of text and cover scan from *Jasper's Beanstalk* by Nick Butterworth and Mick Inkpen © 1992, Nick Butterworth and Mick Inkpen (1992, Picture Knight).
- **Little, Brown and Company** for the use of 'Song of the train' by David McCord from *One At a Time* by David McCord © 1952, David McCord (1952, Little, Brown).
- **The Random House Group** for the use of a scanned front cover, text and permission to base activities on the book *Don't Forget the Bacon!* by Pat Hutchins © 1976, Pat Hutchins (1976, Greenwillow Books).
- **Rogers Coleridge and White** for permission to use 'I won't' by Michelle Magorian from *Waiting For My Shorts to Dry* © 1989, Michelle Magorian (1989, Penguin).

Every effort has been made to trace copyright holders for the works reproduced in this book and the publishers apologise for any inadvertent omissions.

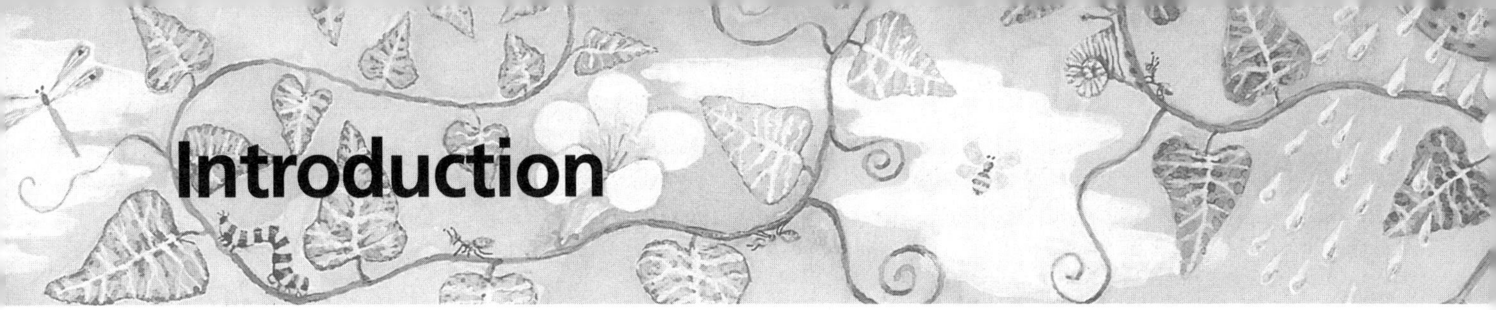

Introduction

Why do I need resources for group time?

The National Literacy Strategy *Framework for Teaching* requires that all children's needs are catered for in the daily Literacy Hour. The class teacher can address individual needs through targeted questions and direct teaching in the first part of the hour when the whole class is taught. However, there is a real necessity for purposeful activities for those children who are struggling readers during the group/independent work section of the hour, when the teacher is working elsewhere with guided reading/writing groups. This book is designed to be used in Key Stage 2 classes, by a classroom assistant or other adult working with a group of children who are reading at Level 1–2.

How does the book work?

Each of the chapters in this book contains five photocopiable lessons, designed to fit into the 20-minute group/independent work slot in the Literacy Hour and to be used by a classroom assistant or other additional adult. The lessons are based on specific texts and children working on the activities will need to have access to them. The three story books are texts at Level 1 (Book Band 5–7):

- *Jasper's Beanstalk* by Nick Butterworth and Mick Inkpen (Hodder Children's Books)
- *Don't Forget the Bacon!* by Pat Hutchins (Random House Children's Books)
- *Not Now, Bernard* by David McKee (Andersen Press).

The children do not need to be familiar with the text beforehand, as the classroom assistant will introduce the story and follow it with a shared reading activity in the lesson for Day 1.

Two non-fiction texts and poems (at Level 1–2) are provided as photocopiable pages. One story or extract is the focus for each week's lesson; the activities are at text, sentence and word level and include writing frames and homework tasks. The homework sheets could also be used independently by the children in class as revision and consolidation.

How does it fit into the Literacy Hour planning?

The learning objectives are chosen from earlier years of the framework, as recommended for pupils working at a lower level than the rest of the class. In most cases, the genre for a particular text will be found in the range for Years 3 or 4, for example stories in familiar settings, stories by significant children's authors, instructions, information texts on topics of interest, poems based on common themes. This makes it possible for struggling readers to be included more effectively in the Literacy Hour. The objectives are clearly indicated in the grid at the start of each chapter, allowing for simple group target-setting.

How flexible is it?

Each chapter in this book can be used independently – there is no need to follow any particular order. Although aimed at groups of children in Years 3 and 4, the activities could also be used with older children who have special needs, and are easily adapted for use with an individual child. The 20-minute format makes the activities ideal for the Literacy Hour, but they could equally be used at other times, for additional support.

Will classroom assistants need any training to use the book?

Everything that is needed to carry out the group-time lesson is explained in the straightforward notes for each day. There are also useful hints provided in the next few pages to help classroom assistants support children with reading, writing and spelling.

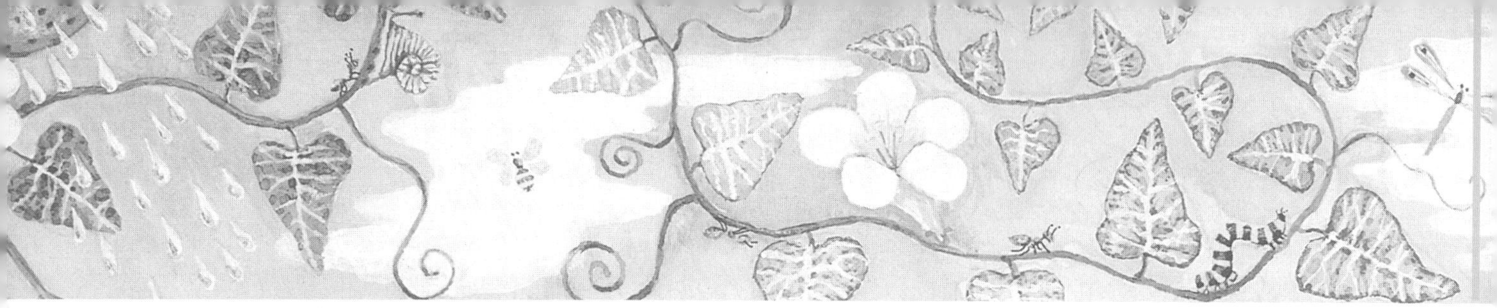

What is the range of the texts?

The three Level 1 fiction texts all fit the genres of stories with predictable and patterned language and stories by significant children's authors. *Don't Forget the Bacon!* could also be used as a story with a familiar setting. Non-fiction texts are instructions ('A recipe for gingerbread') and information ('All about butterflies'). Poetry texts are poems with predictable and patterned language: 'Sand', 'I won't' and 'Song of the train'.

What objectives are covered?

Learning objectives include:

- **Text level:** predicting content, comprehension, sequencing, story writing, story settings, rhyme, rhythm, writing poems, reading and writing instructions, features of non-fiction, alphabetical order, key words
- **Sentence level:** commas, speech marks, verbs, punctuation in reading
- **Word level:** spelling by analogy, high-frequency words, initial and final phonemes, consonant clusters, new vocabulary.

High-frequency words/spelling by analogy

The following lists show the high-frequency words (from the National Literacy Strategy lists for Reception and Years 1 to 2) and spelling patterns (relating to phonics and spelling work for Years 1 and 2) that can be focused on when you are using the activities for each text.

	High-frequency words	Spelling patterns
Jasper's Beanstalk	make	-ay
Don't Forget the Bacon!	for, get	-ake
Not Now, Bernard	now	-ate
Poems with predictable and patterned language	know	-and
A recipe for gingerbread	put	-all
All about butterflies	very	-est

Resources

A Big Book is useful for the introduction and shared reading of the fiction texts, but individual books could be used. A dry-wipe board or flip chart large enough to use with a group is an invaluable resource.

Reading

Before choosing a week's lessons, make sure the text being used is at an appropriate reading level (most children in the group should be able to read it with no more than one error in every ten words).

Children who are struggling readers in Key Stage 2 classes require support in their journey to independent reading. This can be thought of as providing a scaffold which is removed one piece at a time until they are confident to try reading a text by themselves.

Introducing the text: Clear guidance is provided in each chapter for introducing individual texts. At this stage, the children are familiarised with the story and encouraged to find a few key words.

Shared reading: At the second stage of the process, children join in with as much of the text as they are able, particularly any predictable and repeated phrases.
Independent reading: Finally, children tackle the text independently, often with the support of another child.
Consolidating reading skills: Day 2 always includes a re-reading of the now familiar text. It is easier for struggling readers to develop fluent and expressive reading on familiar texts.

Helping children with reading

Ask the children to tell you how they can work out a word they are finding difficult to read. They could:

- go back to the beginning of the sentence
- say the first sound and think of a word that fits
- leave out the difficult word, read a few more words, then have another try
- look for a little word they know inside the difficult word, for example *__gran__dad*
- look for a pattern they know, for example *old* in *t__old__*

Remind the children of things they should ask themselves as they are reading:

- Does it make sense?
- Does it sound right?
- Does it look right?

Helping children with writing

The aim should be to enable the children to write as much as possible on their own, and your help will be geared to developing their skills. The writing frames provided in this book give the children a useful support, so that they are not faced with a blank sheet of paper. Discussion before writing is very important, as struggling readers usually have great difficulty in making the leap between thinking and expressing their thought in writing.

If children ask you how to spell a common (or high-frequency) word that they will need to use again in their writing, teach them to spell it by getting them to write it a few times using the Look–Say–Cover–Write–Check method (see page 6).

Another way to help is to draw boxes for the letters in the word, if it is one that can be 'sounded out' fairly easily. Ask what they can hear at the beginning, middle and end of the word, then help them to fill in the missing letters. For example, if a child wants to write *rocket,* ask him or her to say the word. Any letter sounds the child can hear (typically the *r, k* and *t*) can be written in the correct boxes.

r			k		t

Next, help the child to say the word again, emphasising each sound so that he or she can hear more letters. You may need to explain that there is another letter in *rocket* that sounds the same as *k,* and that the final part of the word *rocket* sounds like *it* but is actually spelled with a letter *e.* Eventually the whole word will appear in the boxes. This technique allows children to feel that they have spelled the word with some help from you, rather than having simply been told the spelling.

r	o	c	k	e	t

Encourage the children to keep on reading their sentences as they are writing them, so that they don't leave words out, or forget what they wanted to say. Remind them about the use of capital letters, full stops and so on, and make sure they read their writing through carefully when they have finished, to check that it makes sense and to see if they can improve the spelling and punctuation.

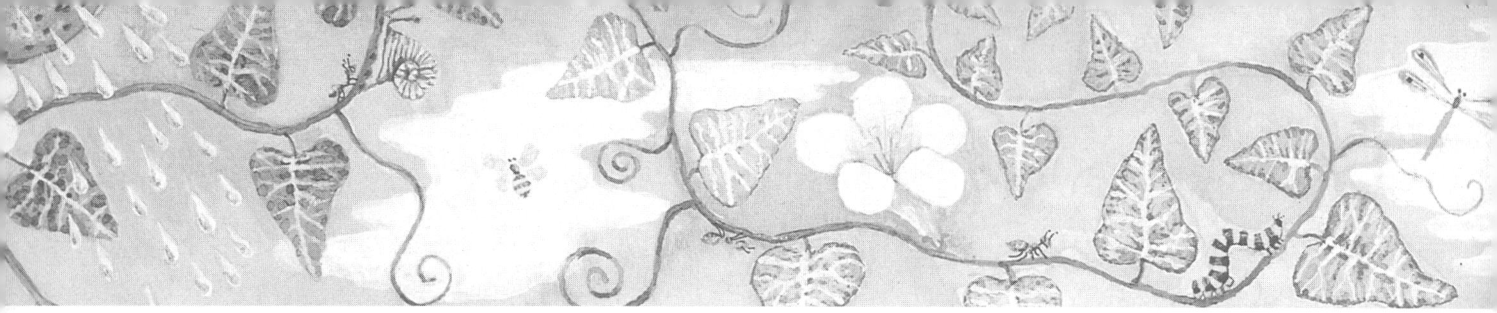

Supporting spelling (Look–Say–Cover–Write–Check)

If you train children to learn a new word by this method every time they want to remember a spelling, they will nearly always be successful.

Have a good LOOK at the word and its shape.
SAY the word and spell out the letters.
COVER the word so that you can't copy it.
WRITE the word down.
CHECK to see if it's right.

The children should repeat the process as often as necessary until they get the word right three times running. Even if the spelling is forgotten later, they will probably have most of the letters right, and relearning will be much quicker the second time.

One reason this method works is because it uses three different ways to learn the same thing. You use your:

- **eyes** to look at the word
- **ears** to hear the letter names as you say them
- **hand** to write the word, and get the feel of its pattern and shape.

This gives the brain several chances to store the word in the memory.

It can help children's handwriting development as well as their spelling if they write the words in joined writing, so that they are learning the spelling patterns as a continuous movement.

Making spelling resources

Some of the activities in this book refer to the use of a word wheel and flick book. These can be made very easily and children really do enjoy using them.

Making a word wheel to learn spelling patterns

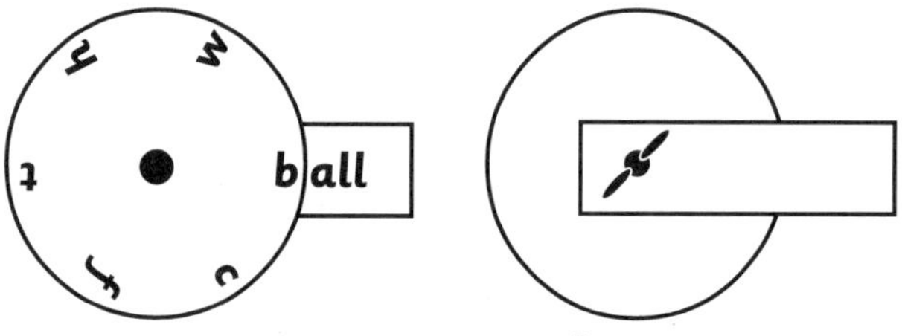

Reverse

Use a butterfly fastener in the centre of the card.

Making a flick book to learn spelling patterns

Staple here.

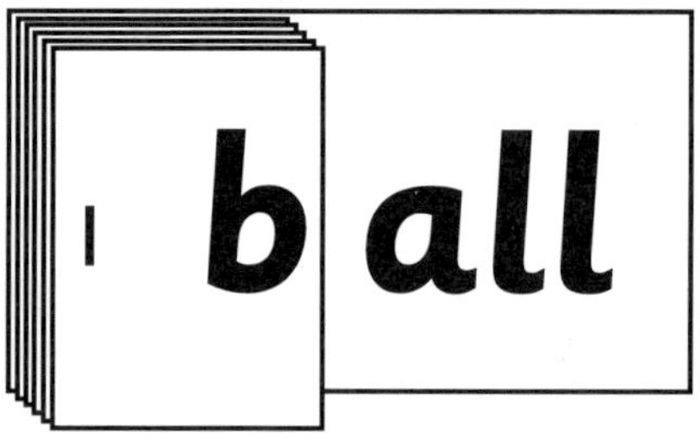

Write a different letter on each small piece of paper to make words, such as *wall, fall, tall* and so on.

Week 1 **Jasper's Beanstalk**

by Nick Butterworth and Mick Inkpen

Introduction

Jasper the cat is determined to grow a beanstalk. One Monday he plants a bean. No efforts are spared in his attempts to lavish loving care on it. Jasper sprays, hoes, rakes and finally mows it, even before it has put out a single shoot. Seriously disillusioned, Jasper digs up the bean and throws it away. Then *a long long long time later* the inevitable happens, and a beanstalk appears, looking uncannily like the picture in the book Jasper is reading about Jack and the Beanstalk.

The day-by-day format of this delightful story provides a simple and repetitive structure that children can use to write their own diaries. The illustrations, which match the text perfectly, will appeal to children as much as Mick Inkpen's popular *Kipper* stories.

Week 1 Objectives

	Word level	**Sentence level**	**Text level**
Day 1 Reading	To learn new words from reading Y2 T1 (10)	To read aloud with pace and expression appropriate to grammar Y1 T3 (3) & Y2 T2 (2)	To use title, cover and pictures to predict content Y1 T3 (7) To use phonological, contextual, grammatical and graphic knowledge Y1 & Y2 (2)
Day 2 Reading Comprehension		To predict from the text Y2 T2 (1)	To make sense of what they read Y1 & Y2 (2)
Day 3 High-frequency words Spelling by analogy	To read on sight and spell high-frequency words from List 1 Y1 & Y2 To recognise words by common spelling patterns Y1 T3 (5)		
Day 4 Phonological awareness	To discriminate words with initial consonant clusters Y1 T2 (3) To identify initial and final phonemes Y1 T2 (1)		
Day 5 Writing			To use story settings from reading to write own stories Y2 T2 (13)
Homework task 1 Sequencing Spelling	To read on sight and spell words from List 1 (days of the week) Y1 & Y2		
Homework task 2 Cloze		To predict from the text Y2 T2 (1)	

Reading

Introducing the story

Look at the cover and draw the children's attention to the:

- title
- author
- illustrator.

Discuss briefly what the story might be about, making sure the children know the names for the gardening tools Jasper is carrying, for example *hoe* and *rake*.

Read the text on the Monday and Tuesday pages of the book to the children, making sure they are following carefully in their individual copies. Alternatively, you could use a Big Book, if one is available.

Ask the children what will follow on the next page (for example, *On Wednesday he…*).

Encourage them to predict what Jasper might do in the rest of the week, and check the illustrations to see if they were right. Stop when you reach *'That bean will never make a beanstalk,' said Jasper.*

Vocabulary

Make sure the children have understood the vocabulary *hoed, mowed, raked* and *sprayed.*

Shared reading

Re-read the text from the beginning, with the children joining in, until the page *'That bean will never make a beanstalk,' said Jasper*. Discuss what the ending of the story might be.

Now read the rest of the story together to see who was right in their predictions.

Day 1 Week 1 **Jasper's Beanstalk**

Resources for Group Time

Comprehension

Reading

Re-read the text all the way through, with individual children reading some pages. (You could allow a less able reader to read in a pair with a more confident child.)

Ask the children what they think will happen next to Jasper. (Talk briefly about *Jack and the Beanstalk*.)

Story quiz (oral answers)

1. When did Jasper plant his bean?
A. *Tuesday.*
2. What did Jasper do on Sunday?
A. *Waited.*
3. What did Jasper say when he dug up his bean?
A. *That bean will never make a beanstalk.*
4. Who climbed up a beanstalk in another story?
A. *Jack.*
5. Why did Jasper pick up the snails?
A. *To stop them eating his beanstalk.*

Story quiz (written answers)

The children could work individually or in pairs, discussing their answers, taking turns to write and helping each other with spelling.

1. What did Jasper do with his spade?
A. *Dig.*
2. Missing word: That bean will never __________ a beanstalk.
A. *Make.*
3. Name one thing Jasper did on Thursday.
A. *Dug/raked/sprayed/hoed.*
4. When did he dig up his bean?
A. *Monday.*
5. On what day did the beanstalk finally grow?
A. *Thursday.*

Day 2 Week 1 **Jasper's Beanstalk**

Resources for Group Time

Sight vocabulary

make

Ask the children to find *make* in the text. Write *make* on a dry-wipe board, with the children spelling the letter names as you write. Ask the children to look closely at the word, count the letters and look for a tall letter.

Say the word and spell the letter names aloud together.

The children should now try to write the word *make* from memory, using the Look–Say–Cover–Write–Check method (see page 6). They could also write the word in their spelling books to take home for revision.

Phonological awareness

Word beginnings game

Ask the children what day begins with *m*. What did Jasper do to his bean on Saturday? *(Mowed.)*

Brainstorm words starting with *m,* then compose a sentence beginning *On Monday morning*, *Mary…* using as many words as possible beginning with *m.*

Spelling by analogy

Spelling pattern: *-ay*

Ask the children to find the word *day* at the end of any of the days of the week in the story. Make sure they can all spell *day,* using the Look–Say–Cover–Write–Check method (see page 6).

Ask the children to suggest rhyming words, for example *play, way, may, stay, say, clay.*

Dictate either or both of the following sentences for the children to write. (Decide if you want them to have the rhyming word list for reference.)

May *we* ***stay*** *and* ***play*** *with you?*
Today *my hen* ***may lay*** *an egg.*

Ask the children to check their sentences, then underline the *-ay* words.

They could make word wheels or flick books with the spelling pattern to take home (see page 6).

Week 1 **Jasper's Beanstalk**

Day 3

Resources for Group Time

Phonological awareness

Slugs and snails game
(consonant digraphs *sl* and *sn*)

Ask the children to find the words *slugs* and *snails* on the Friday page, and tell you how each word starts: *sl* and *sn*.

Help the children to think of other words beginning with *sl*, then with *sn.*

Divide the group into 'slugs' and 'snails'. The 'slugs' should call out their name when you say a word starting with *sl*, and the 'snails' should call out theirs if the word starts with *sn*.

sleep	*snap*	*sneeze*	*slosh*
slick	*snoopy*	*snout*	*sloppy*
snout	*snowman*	*slimy*	*slide*

Word endings: *-ed*

Look through the story together to find words that end with *-ed (raked, waited).* Help the children to notice they are words for something that happened ('doing' words or verbs). Can they think of other words ending with *-ed*? Help the children to find and write a list of all the words in the story that end with *-ed.*

The children could practise reading the words in pairs.

Week 1 **Jasper's Beanstalk**

Day 4

Resources for Group Time

____________________ 's diary

On Monday ______________________________

____

On Tuesday ______________________________

____

On Wednesday ____________________________

____

On Thursday _____________________________

____

On Friday _______________________________

____

On Saturday _____________________________

____

On Sunday _______________________________

____

Week 1 **Jasper's Beanstalk**

Day 5

Shared or independent writing

Explain that *Jasper's Beanstalk* is a sort of diary. Encourage the children to think of a character whose diary they could write, perhaps from a story or TV programme. They could write about a pet, for example, or it could be about a real person. Model the start of the diary by using the children's suggestions and writing the entry for Monday on the board.

Days of the week

Parents – please help your child to read through this Homework sheet to make sure they understand what to do.

Can you remember the days of the week?

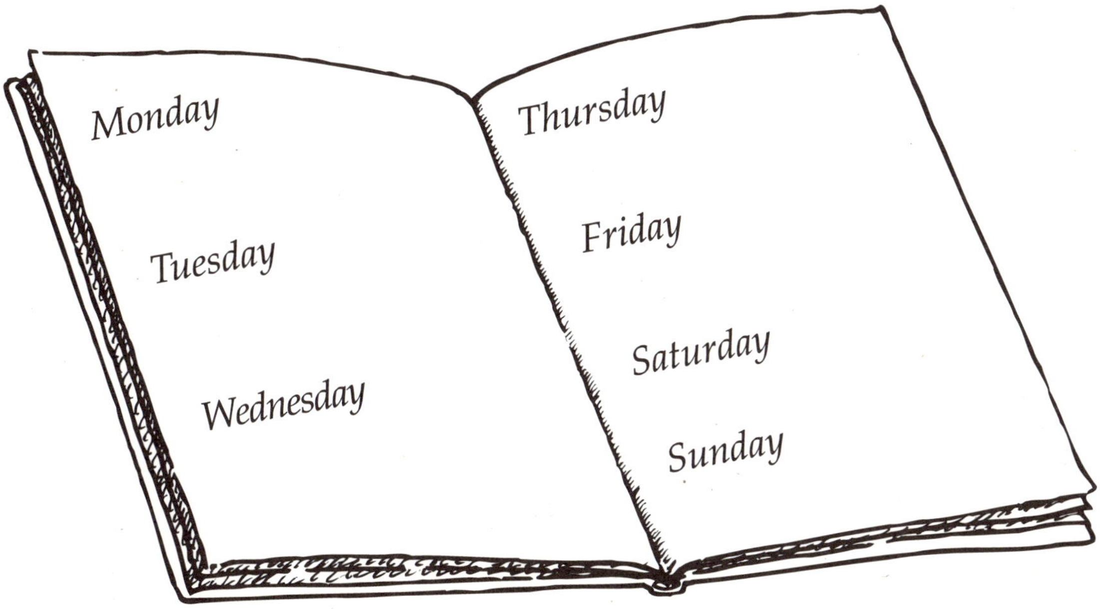

Close your eyes and try to say them.

Put in the missing letters.

Wedne___day **S___ ___day**

Satur___ ___ ___

F___iday **___onday**

Tues___ ___ ___

T___ur___da___

Try to write the names of the days without looking at this page.
How many did you get right?

Missing words

Parents – please help your child to read through this Homework sheet to make sure they understand what to do.

Read the story and put in the missing words from the box in the right places.

On Monday, Jasper found a __________ .

On _______________ he planted it.

On Wednesday ______ watered it.

On Thursday he dug and raked and sprayed _______ hoed it.

On Friday night he picked up _______ the slugs and snails.

Tuesday	all	bean	he	and

Week 2 Don't Forget the Bacon!

by Pat Hutchins

Introduction

This well-known story by Pat Hutchins is about a little boy's difficulty in remembering his mother's shopping list, and the hilarious complications that arise when he substitutes the wrong items. The story provides opportunities for developing an awareness of rhyme and for understanding alternative ways of presenting dialogue in texts, in speech and thought bubbles. The writing frame for Day 5 encourages children's creativity and sense of humour.

Week 2 Objectives

	Word level	Sentence level	Text level
Day 1 Reading		To predict from the text Y2 T2 (1)	To use title, cover and pictures to predict content Y1 T3 (7) To use phonological, contextual, grammatical and graphic knowledge Y1 & Y2 (2)
Day 2 Reading Comprehension		To recognise and take account of commas in reading aloud Y2 T1 (3)	To make sense of what they read Y1 & Y2 (2)
Day 3 High-frequency words Spelling by analogy	To read on sight and spell high-frequency words from List 1 Y1 & Y2 To recognise words by common spelling patterns Y1 T3 (5)		
Day 4 Phonological awareness: rhyme			To identify and discuss patterns of rhyme Y2 T2 (9)
Day 5 Writing			To use structures (rhymes) as a basis for own writing, by substituting and inventing Y2 T2 (15)
Homework task 1 Rhymes			To identify patterns of rhyme Y2 T2 (9)
Homework task 2 Cloze			To make sense of what they read Y1 & Y2 (2)

Reading

Introducing the story

Look at the cover and draw the children's attention to the:

- title
- author/illustrator.

Ask the children who might be speaking the words in the speech bubble *(Don't forget the bacon!)*.

Look at the illustration on the dedication page. What was the little boy supposed to buy? What is missing from the picture?

Look through the book with the children, discussing the muddles.

Stop at the page with the farm eggs and ask the children to predict the ending of the story, then look at the last few pages to see who was right.

Draw the children's attention to the rhymes and the layout of the text in speech bubbles and thought bubbles.

Shared reading

Read the text to the children, encouraging them to join in with as much of it as they can manage. The children should be following the text carefully in their individual copies, as they read. Alternatively, you could use a Big Book if one is available.

Ask individual children to read some of the speech or thought bubbles occasionally.

Independent reading

Re-read the text all the way through, with individual children reading some pages. (You could allow a less able reader to read in a pair with a more confident child.)

Reading

Re-read the story together, with children reading an occasional page individually or in pairs.

Ask them to read a page silently, then tell a partner what it was about.

Make sure they are paying attention to the commas as they read.

Comprehension

Story quiz (oral answers)

1. What was the rake for?
A. *Leaves.*
2. Where did the boy find the rake and the chairs?
A. *In the junk shop.*
3. When did he remember the pears?
A. *At the market.*
4. What kind of eggs did he buy?
A. *Farm eggs.*
5. What did he do when he was wearing the cape?
A. *He rode his bike.*

Story quiz (written answers)

The children could work individually or in pairs, discussing their answers, taking turns to write and helping each other with spelling.

1. Who told the boy not to forget the bacon?
A. *Mum.*
2. How many fat legs were there?
A. *Six.*
3. Who went shopping with the boy?
A. *The dog.*
4. Missing word: Six ________ pegs.
A. *Clothes.*
5. What was for tea?
A. *A cake.*

Sight vocabulary

for, get

Ask the children to find two words that are part of *forget (for* and *get)* in the title of the book. Write *for* on a dry-wipe board, with the children spelling the letter names as you write. Ask the children to look closely at the word, count the letters and look for tall letters and letters with tails.

Say the word and spell the letter names aloud together.

The children should now try to write the word *for* from memory, using the Look–Say–Cover–Write–Check method until they are confident (see page 6). They could also write the word in their spelling books to take home for revision.

Follow the same procedure with *get.*

Spelling by analogy

Spelling pattern: *-ake*

Ask the children to find the word *cake* in the story. Make sure they can all spell *cake,* using the Look–Say–Cover–Write–Check method (see page 6).

Ask them to suggest rhyming words, for example *rake, take, make, snake*.

Silly words game

Write the following headings on the board: *Real words* and *Silly words*. Ask the children to choose any consonant and put it in front of *-ake*, then write it under the correct heading. Add more words ending in *-ake* and read the lists of rhyming words together.

Dictate the following sentence for the children to write. (Decide if you want them to have the rhyming word list for reference.)

We will ***make*** *a* ***cake*** *to* ***take*** *to Gran.*

Ask the children to check their sentences, then underline the *-ake* words.

They could make word wheels or flick books with the spelling pattern to take home (see page 6).

Phonological awareness

Pears and cakes game (rhyming words)

Ask the children to remember the muddles in the story for the *pears* (*chairs* and *stairs*). Remind them of the rhymes for *cake* (from Day 3).

Divide the children into two groups: 'pears' and 'cakes'. As you say each of the words below, the children should listen for words that rhyme, and respond by calling out either 'pears' or 'cakes'.

chairs	*tears*	*takes*	*spares*
shakes	*wears*	*dares*	*wakes*
makes	*shares*	*flakes*	*lakes*

Rhymes

The memory game

Ask the children to tell you what the first three items in the boy's shopping list were. Write them as headings across the top of the board: *six farm eggs, a cake for tea, a pound of pears.* (They could write them in their books.)

Look through the book together, asking the children to find the muddled rhyming items, and to decide in which list they belong.

If there is time, the children could think of more rhyming muddles.

Day 5

Shared or independent writing

Explain to the children that they are going to write their own story about a shopping muddle. Read the shopping list (above) first. Encourage the children to think of rhymes for each item, for example *a can of coke – a funny joke,* then help them to complete the thought bubbles individually.

Rhymes

Parents – please help your child to read through this Homework sheet to make sure they understand what to do.

Draw lines to join the rhymes.

six farm eggs

a pound of pears

a can of coke

food for the cat

a cake for tea

a pile of chairs

a silly joke

a cape for me

six fat legs

a big red hat

How does it end?

Parents – please help your child to read through this Homework sheet to make sure they understand what to do.

Choose the correct word.

tea leaves gardens

1. The rake was for ________________

bears pears pizza

2. A pound of ________________

eggs legs pegs

3. Six farm ________________

joke poke coke

4. A can of ________________

mat cat hat

5. Food for the ________________

Week 3 Not Now, Bernard

by David McKee

Introduction

David McKee's story about Bernard, the boy with the alter ego of a monster, has been popular with both children and adults since 1980. It is a story that can be read at different levels. In one sense, it is a rather chilling tale of unfeeling parents and a neglected child; at another it deals with the monstrous rage felt by many children when frustrated in their dealings with an adult world. It provides a useful opportunity for understanding what is only inferred by the author and not directly stated. Children need to be able to 'read between the lines' in order to fully appreciate the subtlety of the message.

Week 3 Objectives

	Word level	Sentence level	Text level
Day 1 Reading		To identify speech marks in reading Y2 T2 (6)	To use title, cover and pictures to predict content Y1 T3 (7) To use phonological, contextual, grammatical and graphic knowledge Y1 & Y2 (2)
Day 2 Reading Comprehension			To make sense of what they read Y1 & Y2 (2)
Day 3 High-frequency words Spelling by analogy	To read on sight and spell high-frequency words from List 1 Y1 & Y2 To recognise words by common spelling patterns Y1 T3 (5) To identify initial phonemes Y1 T2 (1)		
Day 4 Speech marks Verbs		To read aloud with intonation and expression appropriate to the punctuation Y2 T2 (2) Collect examples of verbs from reading Y3 T1 (3)	
Day 5 Writing			To write simple playscripts based on own reading Y3 T1 (15)
Homework task 1 Sentence order			To make sense of what they read Y1 & Y2 (2)
Homework task 2 Cloze		To predict from the text, read on, leave a gap and re-read Y2 T2 (1)	

Week 3 **Not Now, Bernard**

Day 1

Reading

Introducing the story

Look at the cover and draw the children's attention to the:

- title
- author/illustrator.

Ask the children about the characters on the cover.

- Which one is Bernard?
- Who is the other character?
- What kind of things might he do in the story?

Look through the story together, encouraging the children to predict what will happen before you turn each page.

Stop at the page that shows the monster going up to bed. Ask each child to say what they think will happen and how the story will end. Continue looking through the story to see if anyone correctly guessed the ending.

Shared reading

Read the text to the children, encouraging them to join in with as much of it as they can manage. The children should be following the text as they read, by pointing to the words in their copies. Alternatively, you could use a Big Book, if one is available.

Ask the children to point to the speech marks on one page. Make sure they understand that they indicate the words spoken by one of the characters. (You could explain them as 'talking marks'.)

Ask each child in turn to find examples of words in speech marks and to read the words aloud as if they were the character in the story, with appropriate expression.

Resources for Group Time

Week 3 **Not Now, Bernard**

Day 2

Reading

Re-read the story together, with individual children speaking the words of Bernard, Mum, Dad and the monster. Make sure they are reading with appropriate expression.

Comprehension

Story quiz (oral answers)

1. What did the monster eat?

A. *Bernard's dinner.*

2. Where did Mum put the dinner?

A. *In front of the television.*

3. Where did Bernard meet the monster?

A. *In the garden.*

4. What happened when Bernard met the monster?

A. *The monster ate him up.*

5. Who said 'ROAR'?

A. *The monster/Bernard.*

Story quiz (written answers)

The children could work individually or in pairs, discussing their answers, taking turns to write and helping each other with spelling.

1. Who painted the wall?

A. *Mum.*

2. Did the monster drink tea in bed?

A. *No.*

3. Who hit his finger with a hammer?

A. *Dad.*

4. What did the monster break?

A. *A toy.*

5. Missing word: Go to __________. I've taken up your milk.

A. *Bed.*

Resources for Group Time

Sight vocabulary

now

Ask the children to find *now* in the text. Write *now* on a dry-wipe board, with the children spelling the letter names as you write. Ask the children to look closely at the word and count the letters.

Say the word and spell the letter names aloud together.

In pairs, taking turns, each child can practise tracing the word on their partner's back while saying the letter names aloud.

The children should now try to write the word *now* from memory, using the Look–Say–Cover–Write–Check method (see page 6). They could also write the word in their spelling books to take home for revision.

Phonological awareness

Word beginnings game

Ask the children to think of other words that begin like *now*, with the letter *n*. Make sure they all know the phoneme (sound) for the letter.

Brainstorm words starting with *n*, then compose a sentence beginning *'Not now, Natalie,' said Ned. 'Never…'* containing as many words as possible starting with *n*.

Spelling by analogy

Spelling pattern: *-ate*

Ask the children to find the word *ate* in the story. Make sure they can all spell *ate*, using the Look–Say–Cover–Write–Check method (see page 6).

Ask the children to suggest rhyming words, for example *late, date, mate, gate, hate.*

Silly words game

Write the following headings on a dry-wipe board: *Real words* and *Silly words*. Ask the children to choose any consonant and put it in front of *-ate*, then write it under the correct heading. Add more words ending in *-ate* and read the list of rhyming words together.

Dictate the following sentence for the children to write. (Decide if you want them to have the rhyming word list for reference.)

*I **ate** up all the **dates** on my **plate**.*

Ask the children to check their sentences, then underline the *-ate* words.

They could make word wheels or flick books with the spelling pattern to take home (see page 6).

Week 3 **Not Now, Bernard**

Day 3

Resources for Group Time

Speech marks

Ask the children how readers know when someone is talking in a story. Make sure they notice the 'talking marks' and know the correct term: *speech marks*. You could help them to remember them as '66 and 99' (the shape of the marks).

Read two or three pages aloud together, with a change in tone and expression when someone is speaking.

Ask individual children to choose another page with speech marks and read it aloud, showing a change of voice when the words are in speech marks.

Each child should choose a sentence or phrase in speech marks from the story and carefully copy it, making sure the speech marks are correctly placed.

Verbs

Ask the children to find words in the text that describe what the monster did. Help them to make a list: *ate, bit, read, went, watched, broke, said*.

Make sure the children know that the term for words that tell us what someone is doing is *verbs*.

Now ask them to pretend to be the monster and say what they are doing. For example:

*'I'm **eating** Bernard.'*
*'I'm **going** indoors.'*

They could write down their sentences and underline the verb in each one.

Week 3 **Not Now, Bernard**

Day 4

Resources for Group Time

Not now, Bernard

MOTHER: **Go to bed. I've taken up your milk.**

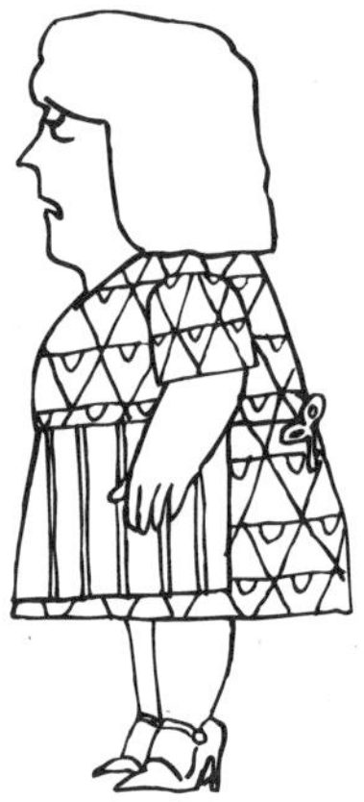

MONSTER: **But I'm a monster.**

MOTHER: **Not now, Bernard**

The next morning…

Writing composition

Explain to the children that they are going to write a play based on *Not Now, Bernard*, starting from where the monster goes to bed, and continuing into the next day. Discuss their ideas first. Who will wake up in the bed – Bernard or the monster? Will anything be different? What will the characters say?

Story jumble

Parents – please help your child to read through this Homework sheet to make sure they understand what to do.

These sentences from *Not Now, Bernard* have become mixed up.
Try to write them in the right order.

1. **The monster ate Bernard up, every bit.**
2. **"Not now, Bernard," said Bernard's mum.**
3. **"Hello, Mum," said Bernard.**
4. **Then the monster went indoors.**
5. **Bernard went into the garden.**
6. **"ROAR," went the monster.**

1. ______________________________

2. ______________________________

3. ______________________________

4. ______________________________

5. ______________________________

6. ______________________________

Homework

Not Now, Bernard

Missing words

Parents – please help your child to read through this Homework sheet to make sure they understand what to do.

Read the story and put the missing words from the box in the right places.

mother	now	garden	father
going	bit	said	monster

"Hello, Dad," said Bernard.

"Not now, Bernard," said his ______________.

"Hello, Mum," ______________ Bernard.

"Not now, Bernard," said his ______________.

"There's a monster in the garden and it's ______________ to eat me," said Bernard.

"Not ______________, Bernard," said his mother.

So Bernard went into the ______________ and the monster ate him up.

Then the ______________ roared at Bernard's mother and ______________ Bernard's father on the leg.

Homework

Week 4 Poems with predictable and patterned language

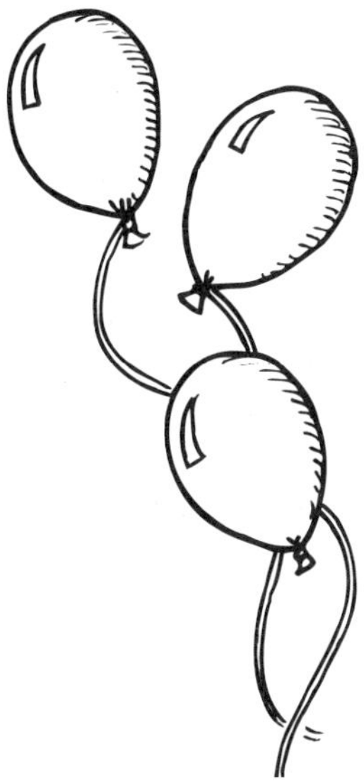

Introduction

The three poems selected for this poetry section all demand to be recited or read aloud. The repetitive format of 'Sand', the insistent rhythms of 'I won't' and the onomatopoeic language of 'Song of the train' make them particularly suitable as poems to be learned by heart or for performance. The use of predictable and patterned language makes it easier for children to access texts that would otherwise be beyond their reading ability.

Week 4 Objectives

	Word level	Sentence level	Text level
Day 1 Reading		To read aloud with intonation and expression Y2 T2 (2)	To identify and discuss patterns of rhyme and rhythm Y2 T2 (9)
Day 2 Comprehension			To make sense of what they read Y1 & Y2 (2)
Day 3 High-frequency words Spelling by analogy	To read on sight and spell high-frequency words from List 1 Y1 & Y2 To recognise words by common spelling patterns Y1 T3 (5)		
Day 4 Contracted words Rhymes	To use word endings *(n't)* to support reading and spelling Y2 T1 (7)		To identify and discuss patterns of rhyme Y2 T2 (9)
Day 5 Writing			To use structures from poems as a basis for writing Y2 T2 (15)
Homework task 1 Cloze		To predict from the text, read on, leave a gap and re-read Y2 T2 (1)	
Homework task 2 Cloze (rhymes)			To make sense of what they read Y1 & Y2 (2)

Week 4 Poems with predictable and patterned language

Day 1

Reading

Introducing the poems

Look at the three poems on photocopiable pages 43 and 44 with the children, and talk about the way the text is organised.

Ask them how they can tell whether the text is a story, non-fiction or poems. Encourage them to say why they know. (The layout is in short lines.)

Shared reading

Look at 'Sand', drawing the children's attention to the repeated words: *Sand in your…* Read the poem to the children, encouraging them to join in as much as possible. Make sure they are following the text as they read, by pointing to the words in their copies. Discuss the experience that the poem is about (playing on the beach).

Read 'I won't', to the children, with expression appropriate to a stubborn toddler, encouraging them to follow in their copies and to join in. Ask the children who the poet was imagining herself to be, when she wrote 'I won't'. Discuss their memories of similar situations (either their own memories or those of younger brothers and sisters).

Read the last poem, 'Song of the train', to the children, and ask them which part of the poem has the strongest rhythm (the *clickety-clack* chorus).

Ask the children what the repeated *clickety-clacks* in the poem sound like (the noise of the train's wheels on the tracks). Tell them the name for a repeated phrase in a poem (chorus).

Read the poem again, with the children joining in as much as possible.

Independent reading

Ask the children to choose their favourite poem. In pairs or small groups, they could read their choice to the group.

Resources for Group Time

Week 4 Poems with predictable and patterned language

Day 2

Comprehension (memory skills)

Re-read the 'Sand' poem together. Now ask the children to turn over their copies of the poems. Read 'Sand' aloud, pausing at the end of each verse for the children to supply the missing rhyming word.

Ask the children if they can remember the rhymes in the poem for *toes (nose), bananas (pyjamas), hair (everywhere).*

Comprehension

'Sand' quiz (oral answers)

1. Where on your head might the sand get?

A. *In your earholes and up your nose.*

2. What might happen when you go to sleep?

A. *Sand could be in your bed and pyjamas.*

3. What food in the poem sounds like it should have sand in it?

A. *Sandwiches.*

4. What footwear in the poem has the word *sand* in it?

A. *Sandals.*

5. Missing word: Sand in your bed at ________.

A. *Night.*

'Song of the train' quiz (written answers)

The children could work individually or in pairs, discussing their answers, taking turns to write and helping each other with spelling.

1. What part of the train goes clickety-clack?

A. *Wheels.*

2. Missing word: *This is the ________ they begin the attack.*

A. *Way.*

3. What rhymes with *back* in the poem?

A. *Clack.*

4. True or false: no one hears the song of the track.

A. *False.*

5. What goes faster and faster?

A. *The song (or the train).*

Resources for Group Time

Sight vocabulary

know

Ask the children to find *know* in the 'I won't' text. Write *know* on a dry-wipe board, with the children spelling the letter names as you write. Ask the children to look closely at the word, count the letters and look for a tall letter.

What small word can they see inside *know*? *(No.)* Make sure they understand the difference between *no* and *know*.

Say the word and spell the letter names aloud together.

The children should now try to write the word *know* from memory, using the Look–Say–Cover–Write–Check method (see page 6). They could also write the word in their spelling books to take home for revision.

Ask the children to suggest rhyming words, for example *land, band, hand.*

Silly words game

Write the following headings on the board: *Real words* and *Silly words*. Ask the children to choose any consonant and put it in front of *-and*, then write it under the correct heading. Add more words ending in *-and* and read the lists of rhyming words together.

Dictate either or both of the following sentences for the children to write. (Decide if you want them to have the rhyming word list for reference.)

*Can you see the **band** on the **sand**?*
*Can I **stand** on my **hands**?*

Ask the children to check their sentences, then underline the *-and* words.

They could make word wheels or flick books with the spelling pattern to take home (see page 6).

Spelling by analogy

Spelling pattern: _-and_

Ask the children to look carefully at the word *sand*. What word is hidden inside *sand*? *(And.)* Make sure they can all spell *sand,* using the Look–Say–Cover–Write–Check method (see page 6).

Week 4 **Poems with predictable and patterned language**

Day 3

Resources for Group Time

Contracted words

Read 'I won't' together, with the appropriate expression, emphasising *won't, don't, hate* and so on.

Draw the children's attention to the word *don't* in the second line. Explain that *I don't* is another way of saying or writing *I do not.*

Ask the children which letter has been taken out of *do not* to make *don't* (the letter *o*). Tell them the apostrophe takes the place of the missing letter.

Help the children to find other examples in the poem of contracted words, with apostrophes (*won't, can't, I'm, it's*). They could highlight them on their copies of the poem.

As each one is found in the poem, write it in a list on a dry-wipe board. Ask the children which two words have been squeezed together for each example. Write each answer alongside the contracted word (*will not, can not, I am, it is*).

Phonological awareness

Rhyme

Read through 'Song of the train' again with the children.

Now ask the children to turn over their copies and listen carefully, trying to put in the missing rhymes while you read it again to them. Miss out the final word of the lines that rhyme with *clack* as you read.

Help the children to find all the words that rhyme with *clack* and to highlight them in their own copies of the poem *(track, attack, crack, back).*

Encourage the children to think of more words that rhyme, for example *sack, smack, hack, black, Jack, lack, pack, quack, rack, tack, stack*. Ask the children to write the words on a dry-wipe board, making sure the *ack* letters are directly beneath each other, so that the pattern can be seen as well as heard.

Week 4 **Poems with predictable and patterned language**

Day 4

Resources for Group Time

I will

I will, yes I will, yes I will do that.

I do want to, I really want to.

Yes I will ______________

I love it. Yes, I love it, yes I love, love, love.

I love to ______________

____

____

____

____

____

____

____

____

Writing composition

Explain to the children that they are going to write their own poems based on 'I won't', but about something they each like to do. Encourage them to talk together first about what they really enjoy doing, and to describe how it makes them feel.

Sand

Parents – please help your child to read through this Homework sheet to make sure they understand what to do.

Some words are missing from the poem. Find the correct words from the list and write them in the spaces.

Sand in your fingernails
Sand between __________ toes
__________ in your earholes
Sand __________ your nose!

Sand __________ your sandwiches
Sand on your bananas
Sand in your __________ at night
Sand in your pyjamas!

Sand in your sandals
Sand in your __________.
Sand in your knickers
Sand __________!

John Foster

hair
everywhere
up
in
bed
Sand
your

Homework

Song of the train

Parents – please help your child to read through this Homework sheet to make sure they understand what to do.

Choose the words to fit the poem.

Clickety-clack
Wheels on the ______________ ,
This is the way
They begin the attack:
Click-ety-clack,
Click-ety-______________ ,
Click-ety, *clack-ety,*
Click-ety
Clack.

back track sack

clack click cluck

Clickety-clack,
_____________ the crack
Faster ____________ faster
The song of the track:
Clickety-clack,
Clickety-clack,
Clickety, clackety,
Clackety
Clack.

Under Over Out

so but and

Riding in ______________ ,
Riding in back,
Everyone ____________
The song of the track:
Clickety-clack
Clickety-clack,
Clickety-*clickety*
Clackety
Clack.

train front middle

hears sees makes

David McCord

Week 5 A recipe for gingerbread

Introduction

This non-fiction text is a useful one for introducing children to the style and format of instructions. Although specialist terms such as *ingredients* and *recipe* are used, the illustrations support the text well, so that the more difficult vocabulary is easily understood by children. The structure of the language used in the text is the same as in many recipes: each instruction begins with a verb telling the reader what to do. On Day 5 children have the opportunity to write their own instructions, with the support of a writing frame.

Week 5 Objectives

	Word level	**Sentence level**	**Text level**
Day 1 Reading Sequences	To learn new words from reading Y2 T1 (10)	To expect reading to make sense and check if it does not Y1 T2 (1)	To read simple written instructions Y2 T1 (13)
Day 2 Key words Reading Comprehension			To scan a text to find key words and phrases Y2 T3 (16) To make sense of what they read Y1 & Y2 (2)
Day 3 High-frequency words Spelling by analogy	To read on sight and spell high-frequency words from list 1 Y1 & Y2 To recognise words by common spelling patterns Y1 T3 (5)		
Day 4 Verbs Instructions		To collect examples of verbs from reading Y3 T1 (3)	To note key structural features of instructions Y2 T1 (14)
Day 5 Writing			To use appropriate register in writing instructions Y2 T1 (18) To write simple instructions Y2 T1 (15)
Homework task 1 Cloze/verbs		To collect examples of verbs from reading Y3 T1 (3)	To make sense of what they read Y1 & Y2 (2)
Homework task 2 Wordsearch	To read on sight high-frequency words from List 1 Y1 & Y2		

Reading

Introducing the text

Look through the recipe on photocopiable pages 45 and 46 with the children, encouraging them to use the illustrations to talk about how to make gingerbread.

Make sure they notice the layout of the text. What do they think the list might be? Why are the sentences numbered? Use the terms *instructions* and *recipe* as you talk and make sure the children understand them.

Help the children to scan the text to find key words such as:

ingredients gingerbread flour
sugar butter eggs ginger
mix shapes oven

Shared reading

Read the text to the children, encouraging them to join in with as much of it as they can manage. They should be following the text as they read, pointing to the words in their copies.

Independent reading

Re-read the text all the way through, with individual children reading different parts. (You could allow a less able reader to read in a pair with a more confident child.)

Encourage the children to think of other examples of instructions, for example school rules.

Key words

Re-read the text together. Children could take turns to read different parts of the text. As you read, help the children to highlight or underline key words about making gingerbread, for example *ingredients, flour, sugar, butter, eggs, ginger, mixes, rolls, shapes, cut, oven.*

Write all the key words on a word web together.

Comprehension

Quiz (oral answers)

1. What is the first thing you do when making gingerbread?
A. *Mix the butter and sugar.*
2. How do you roll the mixture?
A. *With a rolling pin.*
3. True or false: put the gingerbread shapes in the fridge.
A. *False.*
4. What is the last instruction?
A. *Eat the gingerbread.*
5. Why do you roll the mixture?
A. *To make it flat.*

Quiz (written answers)

The children could work individually or in pairs, discussing their answers, taking turns to write and helping each other with spelling.

1. How many ingredients do you need to make gingerbread?
A. *Five.*
2. Do you need cheese?
A. *No.*
3. What do you have to do to the butter and sugar?
A. *Mix them.*
4. How do you make the shapes?
A. *Cut them.*
5. Missing word: Can you ________ a gingerbread boy or girl?
A. *Make.*

Sight vocabulary

put

Ask the children to find *put* in the text. Write *put* on a dry-wipe board, with the children spelling the letter names as you write. Ask the children to look closely at the word, count the letters and look for tall letters and letters with tails.

Say the word and spell the letter names aloud together.

The children should now try to write the word *put* from memory, using the Look–Say–Cover–Write–Check method (see page 6). They could also write the word in their spelling books to take home for revision.

Spelling by analogy

Spelling pattern: *-all*

Ask the children to find the word *all* in the recipe. Make sure everyone can spell *all*, using the Look–Say–Cover–Write–Check method (see page 6).

Ask them to suggest rhyming words, for example *ball, fall, tall, hall, wall, call.* Avoid words that rhyme but are spelled differently (for example *crawl, Paul*).

Ask the children to write them in a list on a dry-wipe board, making sure the *all* letters are directly beneath each other, so that the pattern can be seen as well as heard. Read the list of rhyming words together.

Dictate either or both of the following sentences for the children to write. (Decide if you want them to have the rhyming word list for reference.)

*I put my **ball** in the **hall**.*
*Don't **fall** off the **wall**.*

The children should count the words in each sentence after you have dictated it, and check their own sentences for omissions, punctuation and so on.

Ask the children to underline the *-all* words in their sentences.

They could make word wheels or flick books with the spelling pattern to take home (see page 6).

Week 5 **A recipe for gingerbread**

Day 3

Resources for Group Time

Verbs

Ask the children to find words in the text that tell the reader what actions to carry out when making gingerbread. Help them to make a list:

mix add roll cut put eat

Make sure the children know that the term for 'action words' is *verbs*.

The memory game

Ask the children to try to remember all five ingredients for making gingerbread. Help them to say the instructions for the recipe in the correct sequence, starting each one with a verb. The rest of the group could mime each action as each child gives the instruction. For example, *Mix the butter and sugar together in a big bowl.*

Each child should choose one instruction from the recipe and write it down, without copying. The word web from Day 2 could be used for support.

Week 5 **A recipe for gingerbread**

Day 4

Resources for Group Time

Instructions

A recipe for a ______________________________ sandwich

Ingredients

____

____

____

____

____

____

____

____

____

____

____

Writing instructions

Explain to the children that they are going to write a recipe for making a sandwich. Start them off by brainstorming the ingredients and making a list together (each child can choose their favourite sandwich filling). Before they start to write the instructions, remind them about making sure each of the instructions begins with a verb (Day 4's lesson). Ask them to remind each other about when to use capital letters and full stops.

Missing words

Parents – please help your child to read through this Homework sheet to make sure they understand what to do.

This recipe for gingerbread has lost all the verbs.
Try to find the correct verbs and write them in the recipe.

You will need: **flour, butter, sugar,**

______________, ginger

____________ them all together.

____________ out the mixture.

____________ the mixture into shapes.

____________ the gingerbread into the oven.

____________ the gingerbread with your friends.

Yum, yum!

cut
eat
roll
eggs
put
mix

Wordsearch

Parents – please help your child to read through this Homework sheet to make sure they understand what to do.

Find each of these words in the wordsearch square.
Colour in each word in the square as you find it.

ginger	the	friends
cook	mix	all
put	in	eat

e	a	t	c	m	i	x
o	g	i	n	g	e	r
f	r	i	e	n	d	s
w	a	l	l	t	h	e
s	h	u	p	u	t	c
c	o	o	k	a	i	n

Week 6 **All about butterflies**

Introduction

By reading and responding to information texts, children become aware of the differences between fiction and non-fiction. This text introduces children to aspects of butterflies and their life cycle. Children can develop at an early stage the skills required to use information texts if they are helped to understand the layout and form of non-fiction texts. This text is divided into clear sections, with captions describing the illustrations, to make this easier. The KWL grid (Day 1) and the writing frame (Day 5) provide children with opportunities to revise and practise the necessary skills for tackling non-fiction.

Week 1 Objectives

	Word level	Sentence level	Text level
Day 1 Reading	To learn new words from reading Y2 T1 (10)	To expect reading to make sense and to check if it does not Y1 T2 (1)	To note differing features of non-fiction Y1 T2 (17) To identify questions and use text to find answers Y1 T3 (19)
Day 2 Reading Comprehension		To predict from the text Y2 T2 (1)	To make sense of what they read Y1 & Y2 (2) To make simple notes (key words) to use in own writing Y2 T3 (19)
Day 3 High-frequency words Spelling by analogy	To read on sight and spell high-frequency words from List 1 Y1 & Y2 To recognise words by common spelling patterns Y1 T3 (5)		
Day 4 Vocabulary Alphabetical order	To learn new words from reading Y2 T1 (10)		To use alphabetical order Y2 T2 (18)
Day 5 Writing			To use language and features of non-fiction texts, eg labelled diagrams Y1 T3 (21)
Homework task 1 Comprehension			To make sense of what they read Y1 & Y2 (2)
Homework task 2 Cloze		To predict from the text, read on, leave a gap and re-read Y2 T1 (1)	

Week 6 **All about butterflies**

Day 1

Reading

Before reading

Before looking at the text on photocopiable pages 47 and 48, begin the KWL grid.

K = Things we **k**now

W = Things we **w**ant to know

L = Things we **l**earned

Things we **k**now	Things we **w**ant to know	Things we **l**earned

You will need to make a large grid, so that the whole group is able to see it.

Read the heading of the first column (Things we **k**now). Ask: 'What do you already know about butterflies?' and write down two or three suggestions. (This can be very simple, for example *Butterflies can fly.*)

Read the heading of the middle column (Things we **w**ant to know). Help the children to think of a few questions, and write them in this column.

Give each child a copy of the photocopiable sheets and read the title together: *All about butterflies*. Make sure they all understand that this is an information (non-fiction) text. How do they know? Ask them how it is different from a story. (Non-fiction is about facts and things which really happen or are true.)

Introducing the text

Look through the illustrations and encourage the children to discuss what they can see. Help them to find the following words:

insect	*nectar*	*antennae*
cocoon	*caterpillar*	*chrysalis*

Encourage the children to understand the meaning of these words from the illustrations.

Shared reading

Read the text to the children, encouraging them to join in with as much of it as they can manage. They should be following the text in their copies carefully as they read.

After reading

The children can make suggestions for information to write in the third column of the KWL grid (Things we **l**earned). They may not have found the answers to their earlier questions, and so could be encouraged to find other books about butterflies, or enlist help in searching Internet sites about butterflies, at another time.

Resources for Group Time

Week 6 **All about butterflies**

Day 2

Reading

Re-read the text together. Children could take turns to read different sections. As you read, help the children to highlight or underline key words about butterflies, for example:

insect	*wings*	*nectar*
plants	*fly*	*eggs*

The children should write all the key words on a word web.

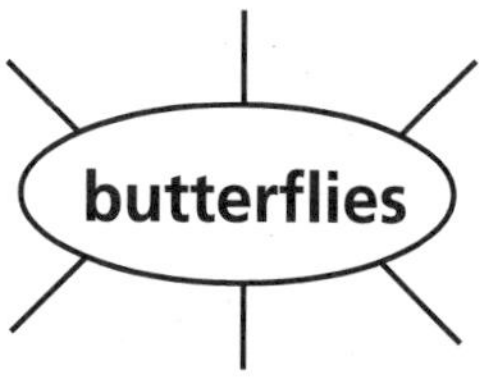

Comprehension

Quiz (oral answers)

1. What is food for a butterfly?

A. *Nectar.*

2. Where does a caterpillar sleep when it is turning into a butterfly?

A. *A cocoon.*

3. True or false: Butterflies live in bushes.

A. *True.*

4. Where do butterflies find nectar?

A. *Flowers.*

5. What comes out from a chrysalis?

A. *A butterfly.*

Resources for Group Time

Sight vocabulary

very

Ask the children to find *very* in the text. Write *very* on a dry-wipe board, with the children spelling the letter names as you write. Ask the children to look closely at the word, count the letters and look for a letter with a tail.

Say the word and spell the letter names aloud together.

The children should now try to write the word *very* from memory, using the Look–Say–Cover–Write–Check method (see page 6). They could also write the word in their spelling books to take home for revision.

Spelling by analogy

Spelling pattern: *-est*

Ask the children to find the word *rest.* Make sure they can all spell *rest,* using the Look–Say–Cover–Write–Check method.

Encourage them to suggest words that rhyme with *rest*, for example *best, test, crest, nest, pest, west.* Write them in a list on a dry-wipe board and read the list of rhyming words together.

Dictate either or both of the following sentences for the children to write. (Decide if you want them to have the rhyming word list for reference.)

She did her ***best*** *in the* ***test****.*
The ***nest*** *was the* ***best*** *in the* ***west****.*

Ask the children to check their sentences, then underline the *-est* words.

They could make word wheels or flick books with the spelling pattern to take home (see page 6).

Alphabetical order

Revise the order of letters in the alphabet by reciting or singing the alphabet with the children.

Butterfly alphabet

Each child should write the first six letters, *A B C D E F*, down the left-hand side of a sheet of paper.

Working as a group, help the children to search the 'All about butterflies' text to find a word beginning with each letter, for example *are, butterfly, caterpillar, different, energy, fly*.

Recite the alphabet with the children again, as they write the letters after *f.* Each child should continue to find and write words to match the letters. Make sure they are able to read all the words. (NB. There are no words beginning with *k, q, u, x, y* or *z*.)

Vocabulary

Ask the children to find *nectar* in the text. Make sure they can all remember what *nectar* means (the butterfly's food, the sweet juice found inside flowers).

Write the word *nectar* on a dry-wipe board, large enough for all the children to see it. Now add the words *caterpillar*, *insect, antennae* and *hatches*.

Read the following descriptions in turn. Ask the children to decide which word from the list on the board fits each description, and to write down their answers.

1. The creature, like a worm, that hatches from a butterfly's egg.
2. The feelers on a butterfly's head.
3. The juice inside a flower that is food for butterflies.
4. A creature with six legs.
5. An egg breaking open, so that a new creature can come out.

What do the pictures say?

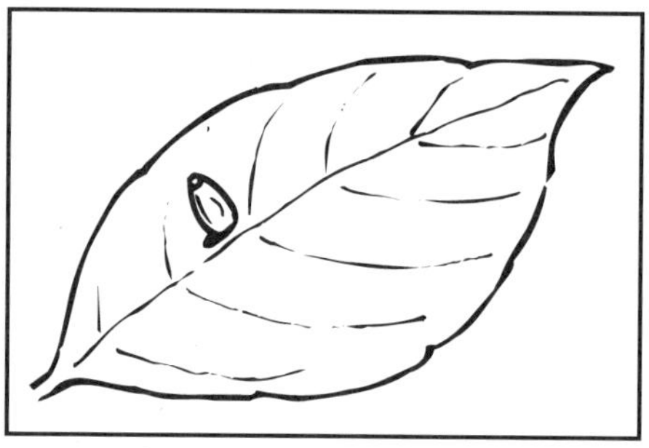

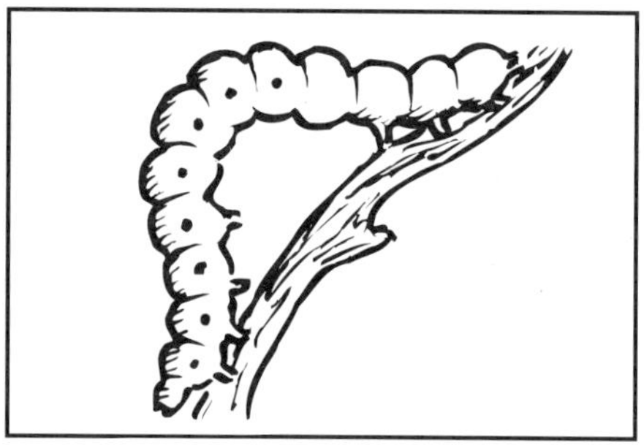

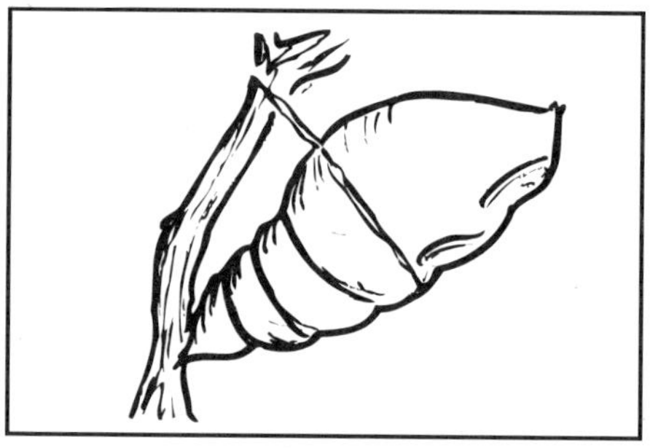

Week 6 **All about butterflies**

Day 5

Writing composition

Look with the children at the illustrations above. Using the KWL grid from Day 1 and the word web from Day 2, help the children to write their own sentences as captions for each illustration. (Remind them first about capital letters and full stops.)

Parents – please help your child to read through this Homework sheet to make sure they understand what to do.

Yes or no?

How much can you remember about butterflies?
Answer yes or no.

1. **Butterflies eat flowers.** ☐
2. **Butterflies come from caterpillars.** ☐
3. **Butterflies live in nests.** ☐
4. **Butterflies have six legs.** ☐
5. **Butterflies grow big.** ☐
6. **Caterpillars can fly.** ☐
7. **Butterflies have two wings.** ☐

Missing words

Parents – please help your child to read through this Homework sheet to make sure they understand what to do.

Read the text and put the missing words from the box in the right places.

A butterfly is an insect. It has ________ wings and six legs. Butterflies rest ______ plants. Sometimes ________ hide in trees. A ______________ feeds on nectar. The butterfly sucks up the ____________ from flowers. When a butterfly lays an ________, it hatches into a caterpillar.

egg	**they**	**nectar**
four	**butterfly**	**on**

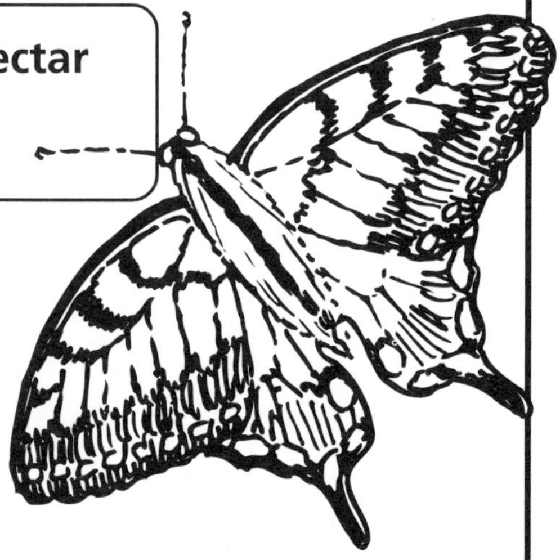

Now try to read the whole text by yourself.

I won't

I won't, no I won't, no I won't do that.
I don't want to, I don't have to,
No I won't wear that hat.
I hate it, yes I hate it, yes I hate hate hate.
You can't make me, I don't want to,
I don't care if we are late.
Yes I'm naughty, yes I'm naughty,
Yes I know, know, know.
But I won't wear that hat
So it's No! No! No!

Michelle Magorian

Sand

Sand in your fingernails
Sand between your toes
Sand in your earholes
Sand up your nose!

Sand in your sandwiches
Sand on your bananas
Sand in your bed at night
Sand in your pyjamas!

Sand in your sandals
Sand in your hair
Sand in your knickers
Sand everywhere!

John Foster

Anthology

Song of the train

Clickety-clack
Wheels on the track,
This is the way
They begin the attack:
Click-ety-clack,
Click-ety-clack,
Click-ety, *clack-ety,*
Click-ety
Clack.

Clickety-clack,
Over the crack,
Faster and faster
The song of the track:
Clickety-clack,
Clickety-clack,
Clickety, clackety,
Clackety
Clack.

Riding in front,
Riding in back,
Everyone hears
The song of the track:
Clickety-clack
Clickety-clack,
Clickety-*clickety,*
Clackety
Clack.

David McCord

Anthology

A recipe for gingerbread

These are the ingredients you will need:

flour
eggs
butter
sugar
ginger

1. Mix the butter and sugar together in a big bowl.

2. Add the eggs and mix it all together.

3. Mix in the flour and ginger.

4. Roll the mixture with a rolling pin to make it flat.

5. Cut it into different shapes. Can you make a gingerbread boy or girl?

6. Put the gingerbread shapes on a baking tray.

7. Put the tray into the oven for 30 minutes.

8. Don't forget to do the washing-up.

9. Eat the gingerbread for tea, with your friends.

All about butterflies

There are lots of different sorts of butterfly. Some have very bright colours, some look like leaves.

A butterfly is an insect. It has six legs and four wings. On its head are two long feelers called antennae.

Butterflies live in plants and bushes. They fly around and then rest on plants. Sometimes they hide in the leaves.

Nectar is the butterflies' food. They find nectar in flowers. It is a sticky sweet juice.

The nectar gives butterflies energy so that they can fly.

Anthology

1. The butterfly lays its eggs on a leaf.

2. The egg hatches out. A caterpillar is really a baby butterfly.

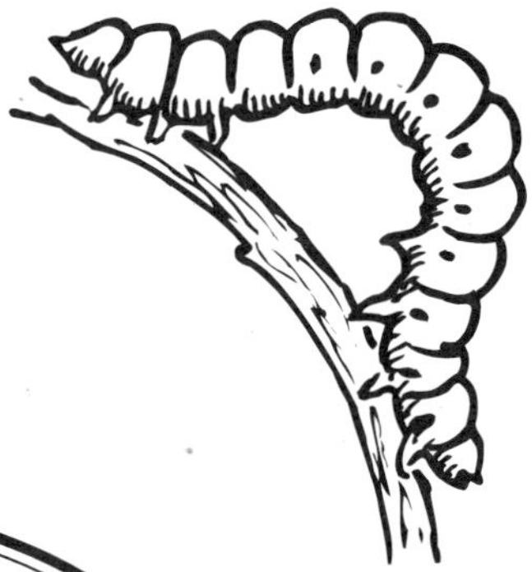

The life cycle of a butterfly

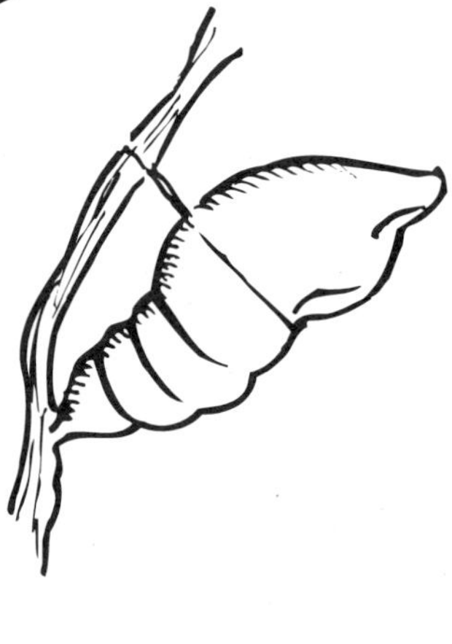

3. The caterpillar makes a cocoon to sleep in. Now it is called a chrysalis.

4. A new butterfly comes out from the chrysalis. Butterflies do not grow. They are adult insects and stay the same size.